This Book Belongs To

Made in the USA
Columbia, SC
02 January 2025

51053289R00067